EASTERN EUROPEAN EATS

REGIONAL DISHES FROM POLAND AND CZECH REPUBLIC

MARITA LUDVIGSEN

outskirts
press

Dedication

I grew up in upstate New York with first-generation Czech and Polish parents. My mother was a great cook who made many traditional old-country dishes. My earliest memories are of my mother cooking in the kitchen and the amazing aromas that floated through the house. She easily put ingredients together which resulted in amazing culinary delights which filled the kitchen with irresistible, mouthwatering smells that greeted my siblings and me when coming home from school. This book is dedicated to her, Marie Mallery, and my maternal grandmother, Elizabeth Zaicek. They both provided me with my Eastern European heritage and my love of cooking. Both of these amazing women could make wonderful dishes out of the most meager ingredients.

These are family recipes handed down over the generations. It is a shout-out to my Eastern European heritage and the many wonderful memories that cooking these dishes invokes. Please understand that the directions are not always extensive, and the quantities produced are sometimes not exact. Having said that, this food created fond memories for our family, and my grown children continue to enjoy making these treasured dishes. I have also added many of the favorite dishes I made for my family of three children over the years. These recipes often came from friends and family members from their own cooking experiences which became part of our cooking traditions.

My hope is that this cookbook will bring a touch of happiness to everyone who tries a new recipe. Experiment with these ingredients to create fond memories for you and your loved ones. Enjoy!

Contents

APPETIZERS

Marinated Broccoli

INGREDIENTS

- 3 bunches fresh broccoli
- 1 cup cider vinegar
- 1 tablespoon sugar
- 1 tablespoon dill weed
- 1 teaspoon salt
- 1 teaspoon pepper
- 1 teaspoon garlic powder
- 1 cup vegetable oil

INSTRUCTIONS

1. Cut flowerets into bite size.
2. Mix all other ingredients.
3. Pour over broccoli.
4. Refrigerate 24 hours.
5. Drain and serve.

Marinated Pretzels

INGREDIENTS

- 1 bag beer pretzels
- 1 dry package Hidden Valley Ranch dressing
- 1 cup vegetable oil
- 1/2 teaspoon dill weed
- 1/2 teaspoon garlic powder
- 1/2 teaspoon lemon pepper

INSTRUCTIONS

1. Preheat oven to 400°F.
2. Break pretzels into bite-size pieces.
3. Stir all ingredients together and add pretzels.
4. Marinate for 1 hour.
5. Bake for 6 minutes.

DRINKS

Brandy Slushy

Russian Tea

Benbreno (soda mix)

Brandy Slushy

INGREDIENTS

- 5 cups water
- 1/2 cup sugar
- 3 tea bags
- 12 ounces frozen OJ
- 12 ounces frozen limeade
- 2 cups brandy

INSTRUCTIONS

1. Boil the water, sugar, and add tea bags to steep; then cool.
2. Mix remainder of ingredients to water mixture.
3. Mix well.
4. Place in container and freeze.
5. As liquid freezes, mix with a spoon.
6. Serve as a slushy or mix with lemon-lime soda.
7. Can triple quantity.

Russian Tea

So great on a cold day!

INGREDIENTS

- 18 ounce jar of Tang
- 3/4 cup instant tea w/lemon & sugar
- 2 teaspoons cinnamon
- 1/2 teaspoon ground cloves
- 1 cup sugar

INSTRUCTIONS

1. Mix all ingredients.
2. Keep in airtight jar with lid.
3. Use 1–2 tablespoons in 1 cup hot water and mix well.

Benbreno (soda mix)

This is a receipt that my grandson, Ben, developed and named.

INGREDIENTS

- 1/2 glass mango soda
- 1/4 glass black cherry soda
- 1/4 glass lemonade
- Dash root beer soda

INSTRUCTIONS

1. Mix all ingredients together and enjoy.
2. This is actually pretty good!

MAIN DISHES

Palachinky (pancakes filled with cottage cheese)
Polish Kiebassi (smoked sausage)
Goulash (beef stew)
Pierogie (filled dough like pot stickers)
Impossible Taco Pie
Chili
Pot Roast
City Chicken
Barbeque Bean Bake
Spiedies (marinated skewers)
Fried Chicken (Southern style)
Plaza Steak Soup
Halupki (cabbage rolls)
Chicken and Broccoli Bake

Palachinky (pancakes filled with cottage cheese)

This is another recipe my mom would use for meatless Fridays.

INGREDIENTS

- 1 cup flour
- Pinch salt
- 1 egg
- Enough milk to make very thin (start with 1/3 cup)
- Cottage cheese sweetened to taste with sugar

INSTRUCTIONS

1. Pour 1/3 cup of mixture into lightly greased frying pan making very large pancake.
2. Turn over quickly.
3. Roll with cottage cheese filling.
4. Serve immediately.

Polish Kiebassi (smoked sausage)

Yield: Many

This recipe brings back fond memories of my dad smoking these links in the backyard in a homemade smoker.

These were the best kiebassi I ever ate!

INGREDIENTS
- 95 pounds ground pork butt
- 5 pounds course ground ham
- 40 ounces Kosher salt
- 10 ounces ground pepper
- 10 ounces brown sugar mixed in 1 quart water
- 2 ounces marjoram
- 10 ounces garlic powder
- 20 ounces minced onions
- 2 ounces Accent

INSTRUCTIONS
1. Mix all ingredients together.
2. Put through a sausage stuffing machine with natural casings.
3. Tie off lengths about 12 inches and make into circles.
4. Hang links in smoker with cherrywood for 12 hours.

Goulash (beef stew)

INGREDIENTS

- 2 pounds cubed beef
- 1 large onion chopped
- 1 clove garlic crushed
- 2 tablespoons vegetable oil
- 5-6 large potatoes peeled and cubed
- 1 pound carrots peeled and cubed
- 24 ounces beef broth
- 1 tablespoon salt
- 1/2 teaspoon black pepper

INSTRUCTIONS

1. Sauté onions and garlic in 1/2 oil until clear; set aside.
2. Brown beef in remaining oil.
3. Add onions, garlic, vegetables, and broth in a large pan; bring to boil, then simmer until beef is tender about 1–2 hours.

Pierogie (filled dough like pot stickers)

Yield: Dozens

This meal was typically made on Fridays during Lent for a meatless meal.

Once made, they can be frozen in the raw state, then defrosted and cooked.

INGREDIENTS
- 3 cups flour
- 3 tablespoons butter
- Pinch salt
- 2 eggs well beaten
- Milk for consistency

FILLING:
- Mashed potatoes with cheese or fried cabbage

INSTRUCTIONS
1. Mix all ingredients together.
2. Add milk until dough is workable.
3. Roll dough out on floured surface.
4. Cut into fillable squares (maybe 3x3).
5. Fill the dough, then pinch together the sides.
6. Drop into boiling water for 3 minutes or until floating.
7. Drain well, put in bowl with butter, and serve.

Impossible Taco Pie

INGREDIENTS

- 1 pound lean ground beef
- 1 medium onion chopped (1/2 cup)
- 1 package (1 ounce) taco seasoning mix
- 1 can (4.5 ounces) chopped green chiles, drained
- 1 cup milk
- 2 eggs
- 1/2 cup Original Bisquick® mix
- 3/4 cup shredded Monterey Jack or Cheddar cheese (3 ounces)
- 1 jar salsa (any variety)
- Sour cream, if desired

INSTRUCTIONS

1. Preheat oven to 400°F.
2. Grease 9-inch pie plate.
3. Cook ground beef and onion in 10-inch skillet over medium heat, stirring occasionally, until beef is brown; drain.
4. Stir in seasoning mix (dry).
5. Spoon into pie plate; top with chilies.
6. Stir milk, eggs, and Bisquick mix until blended. Pour into pie plate.
7. Bake about 25 minutes or until knife inserted in center comes out clean.
8. Sprinkle with cheese. Bake 8 to 10 minutes longer. Cool 5 minutes.
9. Serve with salsa and sour cream, chopped tomatoes, and lettuce.

Chili

Yield: A lot

INGREDIENTS

- 2 pounds coarse ground beef
- 1 large onion chopped
- 1 large pepper chopped
- 1 clove garlic chopped
- 1 jar pureed tomatoes (or sauce)
- 1 large can red kidney beans including liquid
- 3 dried bay leaves
- salt, pepper to taste
- 1 tablespoon paprika
- 2–3 tablespoons chili powder

INSTRUCTIONS

1. Brown meat in vegetable oil, then remove.
2. Cook onions, garlic, and peppers until tender.
3. Add all ingredients to large pot.
4. Add 1/2–1 cup water.
5. Bring to boil, then cook on simmer until thickened about 2 hours.
6. Serve with chopped onions and grated cheese on top.

Pot Roast

INGREDIENTS

- 3–4 pounds rump roast
- 1 large can cream mushroom soup
- 1 dry pack onion soup mix
- 1 can water

INSTRUCTIONS

1. Place roast in crock pot (nice to use disposable liner!).
2. Mix ingredients in bowl.
3. Pour over roast.
4. Cook on high until tender 6 hours or so.

Great with mashed potatoes and a salad!

City Chicken

Yield: Six sticks

INGREDIENTS

- 1 pound pork cut into cubes
- Italian bread crumbs
- Parmesan grated cheese
- Salt, pepper
- 1 egg
- 6-inch wooden skewers

INSTRUCTIONS

1. Preheat oven to 350°F.
2. Place the meat onto the skewers.
3. Beat one egg with 1 tablespoon water.
4. Mix bread crumbs with cheese, salt, pepper.
5. Roll skewers in egg wash, then crumbs.
6. Fry in vegetable oil until browned.
7. Put in small baking dish.
8. Cover with foil.
9. Bake for 45 minutes.
10. Remove foil to crisp.

Barbeque Bean Bake

INGREDIENTS

- 1 pound ground beef
- 1 pound chopped bacon
- 1 onion chopped
- 1/2 cup ketchup
- 1/2 cup barbeque sauce
- 1 teaspoon salt
- 4 tablespoons prepared mustard
- 4 tablespoons molasses
- 1 teaspoon chili powder
- 3/4 teaspoon pepper
- 2 16-ounce cans kidney beans
- 2 16-ounce cans pork and beans
- 2 16-ounce cans butter beans
- 1/2 teaspoon garlic powder
- 1 teaspoon hot sauce

INSTRUCTIONS

1. Preheat oven to 350ºF.
2. Brown the beef and drain.
3. Brown the bacon and onion; drain.
4. Add all remaining ingredients; mix well.
5. Place in baking dish and bake for 1 hour.

Spiedies (marinated skewers)

INGREDIENTS

- 2 pounds cubed pork or beef
- 3 lemons juiced
- 1/2 cup vegetable oil
- 1/2 cup cider vinegar
- 1/2 cup chopped onion
- 1 minced clove garlic
- 1 tablespoon salt
- 1/2 teaspoon pepper
- 2 tablespoons chopped fresh parsley
- dash hot sauce

INSTRUCTIONS

1. Mix all ingredients, then add meat.
2. Marinate for at least 24 hours.
3. Skewer meat.
4. Grill until done.
5. Best served on sliced Italian bread

Fried Chicken (Southern style)

INGREDIENTS

- 1 pound chicken breasts sliced thin
- 1 teaspoon salt
- 1/4 teaspoon pepper
- 1/2 cup flour
- Vegetable cooking oil to fry
- 1 cup buttermilk
- 1 egg

INSTRUCTIONS

1. Soak chicken in buttermilk for 2 hours.
2. Drain.
3. Mix remaining ingredients except egg.
4. Dredge chicken through beaten egg then flour mixture.
5. Fry in vegetable oil until brown and very crisp.

Plaza Steak Soup

INGREDIENTS

- 1 stick butter
- 1 cup flour
- 2 quarts water
- 3 pounds ground beef
- 3 bouillon cubes
- 1 cup chopped onion
- 1 cup cubed carrots
- 1 cup cubed celery
- 2 cups frozen mixed vegetables
- 1 can stewed tomatoes
- 2 tablespoons BV broth and sauce

INSTRUCTIONS

1. Brown beef and drain.
2. Add remaining ingredients.
3. Bring to a boil, then simmer a long time.
4. If you cannot find BV broth, add 2 tablespoons beef concentrate.
5. Freezes very well.

Halupki (cabbage rolls)

Yield: Many cabbage rolls

INGREDIENTS

- 1 large head cabbage1/4 teaspoon salt
- 1 1/2 pounds ground beef
- 1 1/2 pounds ground pork
- 1 cup cooked rice
- 1/4 cup chopped onion
- 2 tablespoons chopped fresh parsley
- 2 eggs beaten
- 1/2 teaspoon garlic powder
- 1/2 teaspoon salt
- 1/2 teaspoon ground black pepper
- 1/2 cup sour cream
- 1 28-ounce jar tomato sauce
- 1 can tomato soup
- 1 cup sauerkraut
- 1/2 pound bacon slices

INSTRUCTIONS

1. Preheat oven to 350°F.
2. Put cabbage head in boiling salted water.
3. As leaves wilt, continue to remove from head.
4. Place in strainer to cool; shave spine off leaves, reserve.
5. Reserve 12-oz. cabbage water.
6. In a large bowl, mix meat, rice, onion, parsley, eggs, garlic, salt, and pepper.
7. Lightly pack a small amount of meat mixture in center of each leaf; fold sides together and roll.
8. Cut leftover leaves and spines into small pieces.
9. Layer cabbage rolls in large roasting pan; cover with pieces and sauerkraut.
10. Mix tomato sauce, cabbage water, tomato soup.
11. Pour mixture over rolls.
12. Put slices of bacon over top.
13. Cover pan with aluminum foil.
14. Bake for about 2 1/2 hours; baste every hour.

Chicken and Broccoli Bake

INGREDIENTS

- 20-oz. fresh steamed broccoli
- 2 cups cooked sliced chicken
- 2 cans cream of chicken soup
- 1 1/2 cups mayo
- 2 tablespoons lemon juice
- 1 tablespoon curry powder
- 2 cups shredded sharp Cheddar cheese

INSTRUCTIONS

1. Preheat oven to 400°F.
2. Put broccoli in 13x9-inch pan.
3. Cover with chicken.
4. Mix liquid ingredients, pour over top.
5. Cover with cheese.
6. Cover with aluminum foil and bake for 60 minutes.

SIDE DISHES

Chopped Salad
Egg Noodles
Drobki (grated noodles)
Onion Rolls
Homemade Bread
Fleki
Grilled Marinated Artichokes
Corn Bread (Southern)
Cuke Cooler
Sweet Potato Soufflé
Knofli (dumplings)
Potato Pancakes (latke)
Yorkshire Pudding (giant size)
Dill Pickles
Pickled Green Tomatoes

Chopped Salad

INGREDIENTS

- Head of Romaine lettuce
- 1 English cucumber
- Shredded carrot
- 1 sweet onion
- 1 sweet pepper
- 1 jalapeno pepper (if desired)
- 1 red tomato
- Dressing
- 1/3 cup balsamic vinegar
- 1/3 cup olive oil
- 1 tablespoon Kosher salt]
- ½ teaspoon ground pepper
- ½ teaspoon powdered garlic
- ½ teaspoon powdered onion
- ½ teaspoon white sugar

INSTRUCTIONS

1. Chop all ingredients for the salad
2. Put the dressing in a bowl and mix
3. Add dressing to salad and serve immediately

Egg Noodles

INGREDIENTS

- 3 cups flour
- 1/2 teaspoon salt
- Enough eggs to make dough stick together

INSTRUCTIONS

1. Combine ingredients.
2. Roll out thin on floured surface.
3. Allow to dry for 4 hours.
4. Lay sheets on top of one another, cut into strips.
5. Add to boiling water until tender; drain, serve with butter.

Drobki (grated noodles)

INGREDIENTS

- 1 cup flour
- 1/4 teaspoon salt
- 1 or 2 eggs, enough to make the dough stiff

INSTRUCTIONS

1. Mix ingredients together.
2. Refrigerate for 4 hours.
3. Heat some soup or broth in a small pot.
4. Grate noodles into boiling soup for a couple of minutes.
5. Place this mixture into your bowl of soup.

Onion Rolls

Yield: One dozen

Brown the onions.

INGREDIENTS

- 1/2 cup scalded milk
- 1/4 cup butter
- 1 teaspoon sugar
- 1 1/2 teaspoons sugar
- 1 package dry yeast
- 1 egg
- 3/4 cup fried onions
- 3 cups flour

INSTRUCTIONS

1. Preheat oven to 400ºF.
2. Mix the dry yeast with the sugar and warm milk.
3. Add remaining ingredients and knead.
4. Shape into tennis ball size.
5. Allow to rise 15 minutes.
6. Let stand 1 hour.
7. Bake for 15 minutes or until slightly browned.

Homemade Bread

Yield: Four loaves

INGREDIENTS

- 40 ounces lukewarm water
- 3 packages dry yeast
- 2 tablespoons salt
- 1 tablespoon sugar
- 3 teaspoons vegetable oil
- 12 cups flour

INSTRUCTIONS

1. Preheat oven to 400ºF.
2. Mix the yeast in 1/2 cup of the lukewarm water.
3. Add all ingredients and mix well.
4. Knead the dough, allow to rise, and punch down twice.
5. Put dough into bread tins covered (maybe 4 tins).
6. Let rise in warm place.
7. Bake 45 minutes.

Fleki

Yield: Enough to serve 4 people.

It consists of small pieces of dough with cabbage.

INGREDIENTS

- head of cabbage
- 3 cups flour
- 1/2 teaspoon salt
- 2 eggs
- Warm water to make a stiff dough

INSTRUCTIONS

1. Cut a head of cabbage into thin slices and fry with butter and salt until tender.
2. Mix remaining ingredients together. Roll dough on floured surface about 1/4 inch thick
3. Cut into strips, then small squares.
4. Place in boiling water until they rise to top.
5. Drain and butter.
6. Put fried cabbage on them and serve.

Grilled Marinated Artichokes

Yield: Four Servings

Can also use herb aioli to dip.

INGREDIENTS - AIOLI
- 1/3 cup stale bread crumbs
- 1/2 teaspoon white vinegar
- 6 cloves garlic minced
- 1/2 teaspoon salt
- 6 egg yolks
- 1 1/2 cup olive oil
- dash hot pepper
- 1/4 cup fresh basil

FOR THE ARTICHOKES:
- 4 large artichokes
- 2 tablespoons garlic powder
- 1 tablespoon onion powder
- 1/4 cup olive oil
- 1/4 cup balsamic vinegar
- 2 tablespoons chopped cilantro
- 1/2 teaspoon salt
- 1/4 teaspoon pepper
- Juice from one lemon

INSTRUCTIONS
1. Boil artichokes until tender.
2. Cut in half, remove chokes.
3. Mix all other ingredients.
4. Place artichokes in gallon plastic bag.
5. Cover with marinade; refrigerate overnight.
6. Grill until browned about 4–6 minutes.

Corn Bread (Southern)

INGREDIENTS

- 8 heaping tablespoons corn meal
- 2 heaping tablespoons flour
- 1/2 teaspoon baking soda
- 1 teaspoon baking powder
- 1/4 teaspoon salt
- 1 tablespoon Crisco

INSTRUCTIONS

1. Preheat oven to 400°F.
2. Mix all ingredients except Crisco.
3. Place Crisco in cast iron frying pan.
4. Add ingredients.
5. Bake until golden brown about 20 minutes.
6. Serve upside down on plate and cut pie-shaped pieces.

Cuke Cooler

INGREDIENTS

- 1/4 cup vinegar
- 1 tablespoon lemon juice
- 1 teaspoon celery seed
- 2 tablespoons sugar
- 1/8 teaspoon pepper
- 1/4 cup chopped onion
- 2 tablespoons dried parsley
- 3 cukes sliced

INSTRUCTIONS

1. Mix all ingredients together except cukes.
2. Shake well.
3. Add cukes and shake again.
4. Refrigerate.
5. A widemouthed canning jar w/lid works well for storage.

Sweet Potato Soufflé

INGREDIENTS

- 3 cups mashed sweet potatoes
- 1/2 cup brown sugar
- 2 eggs
- 1/3 cups milk
- 1 tablespoon vanilla
- 1/2 cup butter
- 1 cup brown sugar
- 1/3 cup flour
- 1/3 cup butter
- 1 cup chopped nuts

INSTRUCTIONS

1. Preheat oven to 350°F.
2. Mix first 6 ingredients and place in small baking dish.
3. Mix remaining ingredients to make crumble.
4. Top mixture with crumble.
5. Bake for 60 minutes.

Knofli (dumplings)

INGREDIENTS

- 1 yeast package dissolved in warm water
- 3 cups flour
- 1/2 teaspoon salt
- 3 eggs
- Water
- Tomato gravy is tomato juice thickened with roux.

INSTRUCTIONS

1. Mix all ingredients with enough water for consistency.
2. Dough should be firm.
3. Let rise until double.
4. Make into size of snowballs and allow to rise again.
5. Place into boiling water for 20 minutes; don't overcook.
6. Cut in half to check doneness.
7. Serve with tomato gravy.

Potato Pancakes (latke)

INGREDIENTS

- 3 or 4 large potatoes grated (soak in water and drain to remove starch)
- 1 onion grated
- 1 teaspoon salt
- 1 egg
- 1 tablespoon flour

INSTRUCTIONS

1. Mix all ingredients.
2. Make into paddies.
3. Fry in hot greased pan until brown and turn over.
4. Serve with sour cream.

Yorkshire Pudding (giant size)

INGREDIENTS

- 3 cups milk
- pinch salt
- 12 eggs
- 3 cups flour

INSTRUCTIONS

1. Preheat oven to 350°F.
2. Mix all ingredients together; put in large baking dish 9x13.
3. Pour juice from roast beef lightly over pudding; use beef broth if no drippings.
4. Bake until knife comes out clean.

Dill Pickles

INGREDIENTS

- 8 pounds 3–4-inch cucumbers (can be found at farmer's market)
- 3/4 cup sugar
- 1/2 cup canning salt
- 1 quart white vinegar
- 1 quart water
- 3 tablespoons mixed pickling spices
- 2 heads garlic peeled
- Fresh dill (can be found at farmer's market)

INSTRUCTIONS

1. Combine sugar, salt, vinegar, and water in large pan.
2. Tie spices in cheesecloth bag; add to vinegar mixture.
3. Simmer 15 minutes.
4. Pack cucumbers into quart- or pint-size hot mason jars (screw top lids).
5. Put head of dill and one garlic clove in each jar.
6. Fill jar with hot vinegar solution up to 1/4 inch of top.
7. Put on screw top lids.
8. Process quarts in boiling water for 15 minutes. Reomove from water and allow to cool. Yield about 7 pints.

Piccalilli Relish

Yields about 7 pints.

INGREDIENTS

- 4 quarts or about 32 medium cored green tomatoes (farmer's market)
- 2 quarts cabbage (about 1 large head)
- 2 cups sweet green peppers (about 4 small)
- 1 1/2 cups brown sugar
- 1/2 cup canning salt
- 2 tablespoons mustard seed
- 1 tablespoon celery seed
- 1 tablespoon prepared horseradish
- 4 1/2 cups white vinegar

INSTRUCTIONS

1. Chop all vegetables (can use food processor).
2. Sprinkle salt over mixture and mix thoroughly.
3. Let stand 3–4 hours.
4. Drain thoroughly and press to remove free liquid.
5. In a pot, add sugar, spices, horseradish, and vinegar.
6. Simmer 15 minutes.
7. Add vegetables and bring to boil.
8. Pack into hot jars up to 1/4 of top.
9. Adjust lids; process 10 minutes in boiling water bath. Remove from water and allow to cool.

Pickled Green Tomatoes

INGREDIENTS

- 5 pounds small, firm green tomatoes
- 3 1/2 cups white vinegar
- 3 1/2 cups water
- ¼ cup canning salt
- 6 peeled garlic cloves
- 6 Fresh dill heads
- 6 bay leaves

DIRECTIONS:

1. Wash tomatoes
2. Combine vinegar, water and salt in a large sauce pot and bring to a boil
3. Pack tomatoes into hot jars leaving ¼" head space (can half tomatoes if necessary)
4. Add 1 garlic clove, 1 head dill, 1 bay leaf into each jar
5. Pour hot liquid over tomatoes leaving ¼ inch head space
6. Adjust caps to be snug, not tight
7. Process 15 minutes in boiling water bath, take out of water and allow to cool
   Yield about 6 pints

DESSERTS

Rice Pudding

Bourbon Balls

Chocolate Candy Nuggets (cookie crumbs)

Candied Apples

Chocolate Cake

Buthte (nut roll with raised dough)

Monkey Bread

Crumb Cake

Raisin Bread

Red Devil's Food Cake

Peanut Butter Blossoms

Zazvorniki (ladyfinger)

Dark Nut Cake (torte)

Star Cookies with Jelly

Nut Ba Ba (nut loaf)

Plum Pie (paper bag)

Raised Dough Kolache (little cakes)

White Fruit Cake

Carrot Cake

Chocolate Pie Squares

Chocolate Chip Cookies (best ever)

Texas Sheet Cake

Strudel

Brown Sugar Cake

Snowballs

Kolache (filled pastry)

Scandinavian Cookies

Pumpkin Loaf

Prune Cake

Jelly Roll

Boji Milosti (fried dough)

Thumbprint Cookies

Maple Nut Coffee Twist

Rice Pudding

Yield: Very large pot

Can easily cut recipe in half.

INGREDIENTS
- 2 quarts water
- 2 1/2 cups uncooked white rice
- pinch salt
- 2 quarts whole milk
- 2 1/2 cups sugar
- 2 eggs shaken in 1 pint milk
- 1 can evaporated milk
- 2 tablespoons vanilla

INSTRUCTIONS
1. Cook first 3 ingredients stirring frequently until water is absorbed.
2. Add milk stirring frequently until absorbed.
3. Add remaining ingredients and cook until creamy.

Bourbon Balls

INGREDIENTS

- 1 box crushed vanilla wafers
- 1 1/2 cups ground walnuts
- 1 1/2 cups powdered sugar
- 7 ounces bourbon

INSTRUCTIONS

1. Mix all ingredients well.
2. Make into small balls.
3. Roll in powdered sugar.

Chocolate Candy Nuggets (cookie crumbs)

Grandma used cake crumbs to make this.

INGREDIENTS

- 6 ounces semisweet chocolate pieces
- 3 tablespoons corn syrup
- 1 teaspoon vanilla
- 1/2 cup evaporated milk
- 1/4 cup powdered sugar
- 2 1/2 cups vanilla crumbs (or any cake or cookie crumbs)
- 1 cup chopped nuts

INSTRUCTIONS

1. Melt the chocolate.
2. Mix in all ingredients.
3. Let stand until firm.
4. Roll into small balls, then into nuts or coconut.

Candied Apples

Yield: Ten medium apples

Recipe by Grandma Mallery

INGREDIENTS

- 10 medium apples
- 2 cups sugar
- 3/4 cup water
- 1/2 cup Karo syrup
- 2 or 3 drops oil of cinnamon
- Several drops red food coloring at end

INSTRUCTIONS

1. Mix ingredients together in medium pan.
2. Cook over medium heat stirring constantly.
3. Cook to hard crack or 295°F on thermometer.
4. Add color at end of cooking.
5. Wash and dry apples, put in sticks.
6. Dip apples into pan to coat.
7. Place on greased cookie sheet to dry.

Chocolate Cake

INGREDIENTS

- 1 cup flour
- 1 cup sugar
- 4 tablespoons cocoa
- 1/2 cup melted butter
- 1/4 cup sour milk
- 1/4 cup hot water
- 1 teaspoon baking soda
- 1 teaspoon vanilla
- 1 egg

INSTRUCTIONS

1. Preheat oven to 350°F.
2. Mix all ingredients together with mixer.
3. Place equal amounts into two greased small round cake pans.
4. Bake for 30–40 minutes until toothpick comes out clean.
5. Place cooled cake layer onto cake dish
6. Frost top of layer with desired frosting
7. Add second cake layer
8. Frost top and sides

Buthte (nut roll with raised dough)

Watch the baking; not sure of the length of time.

INGREDIENTS

- 1/2 cup warm water
- 1 package dry yeast
- 1/4 cup sugar
- 1/4 cup butter
- 1 teaspoon salt
- 3 1/2 cups flour

INSTRUCTIONS

1. Preheat oven to 350°F.
2. Mix all ingredients.
3. Allow to rise until double.
4. Roll out on floured board fairly thin.
5. Fill with nut filling (ground walnuts, maybe 2 cups with 1/2 cup sugar, enough scalded milk to make a paste—maybe 1/4 to 1/2 cup).
6. Roll and place on greased cookie sheet.
7. Butter top; allow to rise.
8. Bake for 15–20 minutes.

Monkey Bread

INGREDIENTS

- 1/2 cups sugar
- 2 tubs store-bought prepared bread dough
- 1/2 cup chopped walnuts
- 1/2 cup raisins
- 1 cup brown sugar
- 3/4 cup melted butter

INSTRUCTIONS

1. Preheat oven to 350°F.
2. Grease a fluted tube pan.
3. Cut dough into squares; place in rows in pan.
4. Mix all remaining ingredients and pour over bread pieces.
5. Bake for 28–32 minutes or until done.
6. Cool in pan for 10 minutes.
7. Invert pan onto serving plate and enjoy.

Crumb Cake

INGREDIENTS

- 2 cups flour
- 1 cup sugar
- 1/2 teaspoon baking powder
- 1 teaspoon mixed spices
- 3/4 teaspoon salt
- 1/2 cup butter at room temperature
- 3/4 cup sour milk (or put 1 tablespoon white vinegar into regular milk)
- 1/2 teaspoon baking soda

CRUMB MIXTURE:

- 1/2 stick butter
- 1/2 cup flour
- 1/2 cup brown sugar
- dash cinnamon

INSTRUCTIONS

1. Preheat oven to 350°F.
2. Mix all the ingredients together.
3. Place in 9 x 13 inch greased cake pan.
4. Make a crumb mixture of butter, sugar, flour, and cinnamon.
5. Place on top of cake.
6. Bake for 30 minutes.

Raisin Bread

INGREDIENTS

- 6 cups flour
- 1/2 cup butter
- 1 tablespoon vegetable shortening
- 3 eggs
- 2 packages dry yeast mixed in warm water
- 1/2 cup sugar
- 1 cup raisins

INSTRUCTIONS

1. Preheat oven to 325°F.
2. Mix all ingredients together and put in 2 bread pans.
3. Allow to raise until double.
4. Bake for 30–45 minutes.

Red Devil's Food Cake

INGREDIENTS

- 1 stick butter
- 2 eggs
- 1/4 cup cocoa
- 1 teaspoon red food coloring
- 2 cups sifted cake flour
- 1 teaspoon salt
- 1 teaspoon baking soda
- 1 1/2 cups sugar
- 1 teaspoon vanilla
- 3 tablespoons hot coffee

INSTRUCTIONS

1. Preheat oven to 300ºF.
2. Mix all ingredients.
3. Bake in 9x13-inch greased cake pan for 1 hour.

Peanut Butter Blossoms

This recipe came from a friend I worked with years ago.

This recipe can easily be doubled.

INGREDIENTS

- 1/2 cup butter
- 1/4 cup peanut butter
- 1/2 cup brown sugar
- 1/2 cup sugar
- 1 egg
- 1 teaspoon vanilla
- 1 3/4 cups flour
- 1 teaspoon baking soda
- 1/2 teaspoon salt
- 2 bags unwrapped chocolate kisses

INSTRUCTIONS

1. Preheat oven to 350ºF.
2. Cream together butter, peanut butter, sugar.
3. Add remainder of ingredients and mix.
4. Shape into small balls, roll in sugar, then place on greased cookie sheet.
5. Bake for 8 minutes, then remove from oven.
6. Press a kiss into center of each cookie until it cracks, then place back in oven.
7. Bake additional 3–5 minutes.

Zazvorniki (ladyfinger)

This was one of the best things my aunt made! They melt in your mouth.

INGREDIENTS

- 1/4 cup butter
- 4 egg whites beaten
- 1 teaspoon ground ginger
- 4 cups flour
- 8 egg yolks
- 2 tablespoons baking powder
- 1 box (pound) powdered sugar

INSTRUCTIONS

1. Preheat oven to 350ºF when ready to bake.
2. Mix all ingredients; add flour if necessary for consistency.
3. Roll out the dough, cut with cookie cutter (my aunt used a snowman-shaped cutter).
4. Place on cookie sheet; allow to sit overnight.
5. Bake approximately 10 minutes until very light brown.

Dark Nut Cake (torte)

INGREDIENTS

- 9 egg yolks
- 8 ounces brown sugar
- 8 ounces ground walnuts
- 3 ounces dried bread or cracker crumbs
- 9 stiffly beaten egg whites

INSTRUCTIONS

1. Preheat oven to 325°F.
2. Mix all ingredients.
3. Place in a greased bread pan.
3. Bake for 30 minutes.

Star Cookies with Jelly

INGREDIENTS

- 1 pound butter
- 1/2 pound powdered sugar
- 2 lemons juiced and zested
- 4 egg yolks
- 2 cups flour

INSTRUCTIONS

1. Preheat oven to 350ºF.
2. Mix all ingredients together.
3. Start with 2 cups of flour; add more if necessary.
4. Roll onto floured surface to medium thickness.
5. Use star cookie cutter.
6. Bake until golden brown.
7. Cool, spread with jelly, and place second star on top.

Nut Ba Ba (nut loaf)

Yield: One loaf

INGREDIENTS

- 1/2 cup butter at room temperature
- 1 cup sugar
- 7 egg yolks
- 1/2 cup ground walnuts
- 1/3 teaspoon vanilla
- 1 cup flour

INSTRUCTIONS

1. Preheat oven to 300ºF.
2. Beat egg yolks until light.
3. Add sugar.
4. Cream butter and vanilla.
5. Add remaining ingredients together. Place in greased bread pan.
6. Bake 1 1/2 hours and don't test before this time.

Plum Pie (paper bag)

Yield: One pie

This is a fun recipe that keeps your oven clean!

INGREDIENTS

FILLING:
- 4 cups quartered pitted plums
- 1/2 cup sugar
- 1/4 cup flour
- 1/4 teaspoon salt
- 1/4 teaspoon nutmeg
- 1 teaspoon lemon juice
- 9-inch unbaked pastry shell
-

CRUMB TOPPING:
(PICTURED WITH DOUGH TOPPING)
- 1/2 cup butter
- 1/2 cup flour
- 1/2 cup sugar
- 1/2 teaspoon cinnamon

INSTRUCTIONS
1. Preheat oven to 425ºF.
2. Place pastry shell into pie pan.
3. Mix all ingredients except topping and put in shell.
4. Add crumb topping.
5. Place pie in grocery store paper bag.
6. Bake for 1 hour.
7. Remove pie from bag.

Raised Dough Kolache (little cakes)

Filling can be leckvar and/or cottage cheese mixture consisting of cottage cheese, sugar, and raisins.

INGREDIENTS

- 1 cup butter
- 4 cups flour
- Pinch salt
- 4 beaten egg yolks
- 1 cup sour cream at room temperature
- 1/4 cup sugar
- 1 grated lemon rind
- 1 dry yeast package
- 1 teaspoon warm water
- 1/2 teaspoon sugar
- 1 teaspoon vanilla

INSTRUCTIONS

1. Preheat oven to 350ºF.
2. Dissolve the yeast in the warm water and 1/2 teaspoon sugar.
3. Mix all ingredients together.
4. Allow to rise until double.
5. Wrap in wax paper and refrigerate overnight.
6. Make into ping-pong-size pieces.
7. Flatten pieces out and fill with designated filling.
8. Pinch together all sides and place upside down on cookie sheet.
9. Put crumb topping on each (butter, flour, sugar).
10. Allow to rise.
11. Bake for 15 minutes.

White Fruit Cake

This recipe should make 2 loaves. You can certainly cut in half for one.

INGREDIENTS
- 8 ounces each of candied citron, orange peel, lemon peel, and cherries
- 8 ounces pitted chopped dates
- 2 pounds white raisins
- 8 ounces dried figs cut small
- 1 1/2 pounds chopped almonds
- 2 lemons juiced and zested
- 2 teaspoons almond extract
- 1/2 cup brandy
- 1 pound butter room temperature
- 1 pound sugar
- 4 cups flour
- 12 eggs
- 1/2 teaspoon nutmeg

INSTRUCTIONS
1. Preheat oven to 300°F.
2. Mix all ingredients together.
3. Bake for 4 hours.

Carrot Cake

This one is from Grandma Mallery's neighbor, Ellen.

INGREDIENTS

- 1 cup shredded coconut
- 1 1/2 cups vegetable oil
- 1 cup chopped walnuts
- 2 teaspoons baking soda
- 2 cups flour
- 2 cups sugar
- 3 cups grated carrots
- 4 eggs
- 2 teaspoons cinnamon

INSTRUCTIONS

1. Preheat oven to 350ºF.
2. Mix all ingredients together.
3. Place in large, greased cake pan.
4. Bake for 45 minutes.
5. Frost with cream cheese frosting.

Chocolate Pie Squares

Yield: Many

INGREDIENTS

- 1 stick butter, softened
- 1 cup flour
- 1/2 cup chopped nuts
- 8 ounces cream cheese
- 1 cup powdered sugar
- 1 cup whipped cream
- 2 small packages instant vanilla pudding
- 1 small package instant chocolate pudding
- 4 1/2 cups milk
- 1 cup sweetened whip topping or whipped cream

INSTRUCTIONS

1. Preheat oven to 350°F.
2. Mix together butter, flour, nuts.
3. Press into 9x13 pan; bake until brown.
4. Mix together cream cheese, powdered sugar, and whipped cream; spread on cool base.
5. Mix vanilla pudding with 3 cups milk until set; mix chocolate pudding with 11/2 cups milk until set.
6. Spread over mixture.
7. Add additional whipped cream to top.
8. Top with nuts if desired.
9. Refrigerate until cool and serve in squares.

Chocolate Chip Cookies (best ever)

INGREDIENTS

- 1 cup butter
- 1 cup sugar
- 1 cup packed brown sugar
- 2 eggs
- 2 teaspoons vanilla
- 1 teaspoon baking soda
- 2 teaspoons hot water
- 1/2 teaspoon salt
- 3 cups flour
- 2 cups semisweet chocolate chips
- 1 cup chopped walnuts

INSTRUCTIONS

1. Preheat oven to 350ºF.
2. Dissolve baking soda in hot water.
3. Add all ingredients up to flour and beat with mixer.
4. Add flour and mix.
5. Add chips and nuts; mix thoroughly.
6. Drop by large spoonfuls onto cookie sheet.
7. Bake for 10–12 minutes.

Texas Sheet Cake

INGREDIENTS

- 1 cup water
- 1 stick butter
- 4 heaping tablespoons cocoa
- 2 cups flour
- 2 cups sugar
- 1 cup sour cream
- 1 teaspoon baking soda
- 1/2 teaspoon salt
- 2 eggs
- 1 teaspoon vanilla

ICING

- 2 sticks soft butter
- 1 tablespoon milk
- 1 heaping tablespoon cocoa
- 3/4 pound powdered sugar
- 1 teaspoon vanilla
- Chopped nuts for topping

INSTRUCTIONS

1. Preheat oven to 350°F.
2. Mix together first 3 ingredients.
3. Add flour, sugar, sour cream, baking soda, salt, eggs, vanilla and beat with mixer until fluffy.
4. Pour onto parchment paper lined cookie sheet.
5. Bake for 20–25 minutes.
6. Mix together remaining ingredients and beat until fluffy.
7. Spread frosting onto cooled cake; sprinkle with nuts.

Strudel

Yield: Makes 3 loaves

INGREDIENTS
- 3 heaping cups flour
- 1/4 cup butter
- 2 eggs
- 1 cup warm water
- 1/2 teaspoon salt
- 1 tablespoon sugar
- 8 large apples
- 1 teaspoon cinnamon
- 1/2 cup sugar
- 1/2 cup plain bread crumbs
- Powdered sugar when done

INSTRUCTIONS
1. Preheat oven to 350ºF.
2. Mix first 6 ingredients together.
3. Knead 15 minutes until the mixture does not stick.
4. Divide into 3 pieces and place in covered floured bowls.
5. Let stand for 2 hours.
6. Peel and slice thin apples, then coat with cinnamon, sugar.
7. Roll dough out very thin; sprinkle with toasted bread crumbs.
8. Place apples on top and roll dough into loaf.
9. Place on greased cookie sheet seam down.
10. Baste with melted butter.
11. Bake for 30 minutes.
12. Sprinkle with powdered sugar before serving.

Brown Sugar Cake

Many of these old recipes do not have specific directions, only ingredients. This one did not have the baking time or temperature.

INGREDIENTS
- 2 cups flour
- 2 teaspoons baking powder
- 1/2 cup butter softened
- 1/2 cup brown sugar
- 2 egg yolks
- 1 teaspoon vanilla
- 3 teaspoons cold water

INSTRUCTIONS
1. Preheat oven to 350ºF.
2. Mix ingredients including cold water.
3. Put dough into small, greased cake pan.
4. Place 1/2 cup chopped walnuts pressed into dough.

TOPPING—SPREAD ON TOP OF CAKE
- 1 cup brown sugar
- 3/4 cup chopped walnuts
- 2 beaten egg whites
- Instructions

1. Bake until toothpick comes out clean approximately 20–30 minutes.

Snowballs

INGREDIENTS

- 8 ounces butter
- 1/2 cup powdered sugar
- 2 1/2 cups flour
- 1 teaspoon vanilla
- 3/4 cup ground walnuts
- Pinch salt

INSTRUCTIONS

1. Preheat oven to 350ºF.
2. Mix all ingredients, make into small balls.
3. Bake for 12 minutes.
4. Roll immediately in powdered sugar.

Kolache (filled pastry)

Yield: Many cookies!

Kolache is/was one of our traditional Christmas cookies. You can buy Solo filling from the grocery store or make your own. We always used apricot, lekvar, nut meat, and poppy seeds to make ours. All can be made from scratch.

INGREDIENTS
- 16 ounces cream cheese
- 16 ounces butter
- 4–5 cups flour

INSTRUCTIONS
1. Preheat oven to 350°F.
2. Mix dough thoroughly (I use KitchenAid mixer).
3. Start with 4 cups flour; add more if necessary.
4. Make balls the size of large snowballs, then wrap in wax paper.
5. Freeze dough overnight (very important!).
6. Allow to thaw at room temperature.
7. Roll dough out on powdered sugar maybe 1/8-inch thick.
8. Place filling on bottom edge of dough in a line and roll once.
9. Cut into 2-inch pieces and place on cookie sheet; repeat process.
10. Bake for 15 minutes or lightly brown.

FILLINGS FOR THE KOLACHE:
Apricot
INGREDIENTS
- 2 cups chopped dried California apricots
- 1 cup apricot jelly
- 8 ounces water
- 1.2 cups sugar
- 3 tablespoons quick cooking tapioca

INSTRUCTIONS
1. In a medium sauce pan, combine apricots, jelly, water, and sugar and cook over medium high heat constantly stirring until boiling.
2. Add tapioca and reduce heat and simmer covered for 15 minutes. Mixture should be thicker than applesauce.
3. Remove from heat; allow to cool.

4. Pulse in food processor to desired consistency.

5. Chill for up to 1–2 weeks in refrigerator. Can be frozen.

Lekvar (prunes)

INGREDIENTS

- 2 cups pitted prunes, chopped
- 1 cup water
- 1/4 cup orange juice
- 1 teaspoon orange zest
- 1/4 teaspoon salt
- 1/3 cup brown sugar

INSTRUCTIONS

1. Combine all ingredients in saucepan except for brown sugar. Stir and bring to boil for one minute.
2. Reduce heat to low and simmer with lid on for 20 minutes.
3. Remove lid and simmer for 3–5 minutes stirring frequently.
4. When about 3 tablespoons of liquid remains, remove from heat.
5. Stir in brown sugar until dissolved. Allow to cool slightly.
6. Use a masher for immersion blender until puree forms. Run a fork through mixture to break up any pieces.
7. Chill and mixture will hold for 1–2 weeks in refrigerator. Can be frozen.

Scandinavian Cookies

Yield: Many!

These were my favorites from my Aunt Irene. You can make half batches as this is a lot of cookies.

INGREDIENTS

- 1 pound butter
- 4 egg yolks
- 1 cup brown sugar
- 1 pound ground walnuts (use 1/2 for rolling cookies)
- 4 egg whites beaten stiff to roll cookies
- 4 cups flour
- 2 teaspoons baking powder
- 1 teaspoon vanilla

INSTRUCTIONS

1. Preheat oven to 350ºF.
2. Mix all ingredients together.
3. Make into ping-pong-size balls.
4. Roll in egg whites, then nuts.
5. Place on cookie sheet.
6. Bake for 3 minutes then push finger into center to make a well. Fill with jelly.
7. Continue baking for total 10–15 minutes.
8. Cool and enjoy!

Pumpkin Loaf

Yield: One loaf

INGREDIENTS

- 4 eggs
- 2 cups sugar
- 3 cups flour with 3 teaspoons cornstarch
- 2 teaspoons baking powder
- 2 teaspoons baking soda
- 1/2 teaspoon salt
- 2 teaspoons cinnamon
- 1 1/2 cups vegetable oil
- 2 cups canned pumpkin
- 1 cup chopped walnuts

INSTRUCTIONS

1. Preheat oven to 350°F.
2. Mix all ingredients.
3. Bake for 1 hour.

Prune Cake

You should probably use a large cake pan 9x13.

INGREDIENTS

- 2 cups flour
- 1/2 teaspoon salt
- 1 teaspoon soda
- 1 teaspoon baking powder
- 1 teaspoon cinnamon
- 1 teaspoon nutmeg
- 1 teaspoon allspice
- 1 cup butter
- 1 1/2 cups sugar
- 3 eggs
- 1 1/2 cups milk
- 1 1/4 cups mashed prunes

INSTRUCTIONS

1. Preheat oven to 325°F.
2. Cream butter, sugar, and eggs.
3. Add remainder of ingredients.
4. Bake for 25 minutes.

Jelly Roll

INGREDIENTS

- 3 eggs
- 1/2 cup sugar
- 1/2 cup brown sugar
- 1/3 cup water
- 1 cup flour
- 1 teaspoon baking powder
- 1/4 teaspoon salt
- 1/4 teaspoon cinnamon
- 1/4 teaspoon nutmeg
- 1/4 teaspoon cloves

INSTRUCTIONS

1. Preheat oven to 350ºF.
2. Beat eggs.
3. Add sugar, water, vanilla.
4. Add remainder of ingredients.
5. Pour over parchment paper on a cookie sheet.
6. Bake until golden brown.
7. Place hot onto a towel covered with powdered sugar.
8. Spread with jelly when cool and roll.

Sugar Cookies (old-fashioned)

INGREDIENTS

- 1/2 cup vegetable shortening
- 1/2 cup butter
- 1 1/2 cups sugar
- 2 eggs
- 3 cups flour
- 1/2 teaspoon baking powder
- 1/2 teaspoon salt
- 1/4 cup milk
- 1/2 teaspoon vanilla

INSTRUCTIONS

1. Preheat oven to 375°F.
2. Mix all ingredients together.
3. Roll dough on floured surface medium height.
4. Cut dough into round circles.
5. Bake for 8 minutes.

Boji Milosti (fried dough)

Yield: One dozen

Basically, this is fried dough. My mother used to fry it in lard. I suggest using vegetable oil.

INGREDIENTS
- 1/2 pint sour cream
- 4 eggs
- 2 cups flour
- 5 tablespoons sugar
- 1 teaspoon salt

INSTRUCTIONS
1. Mix all ingredients together.
2. Roll on floured board.
3. Cut into triangle shapes and cut 2 slits in middle.
4. Fry in hot vegetable oil.
5. Turn to brown on second side.
6. Cool on paper towels.
7. Sprinkle with powdered sugar.

Thumbprint Cookies

INGREDIENTS

- 2 eggs
- 2 cups flour
- 1 cup butter at room temperature 1/2 cup packed brown sugar
- 1 teaspoon vanilla
- 1/8 teaspoon salt
- 2 1/2 cups finely ground walnuts

INSTRUCTIONS

1. Preheat oven to 350ºF.
2. Separate eggs, beat whites, and set aside.
3. Mix all other ingredients in bowl; beat at low speed until it forms a dough.
4. Shape a rounded tablespoon dough into 1-inch balls.
5. Roll in egg white and then in nuts.
6. Place 1 inch apart on greased cookie sheet.
7. Make indentations in center each cookie.
8. Bake for 8 minutes.
9. Remove from oven and fill each cookie with jelly.
10. Continue baking 6–10 minutes until brown.

Maple Nut Coffee Twist

INGREDIENTS

- 1 pkg. hot roll mix
- 3/4 cup very warm water
- 1 egg
- 3 tablespoons sugar
- 1 teaspoon maple flavoring

FILLING:

INGREDIENTS

- 1/2 cup sugar
- 1 teaspoon cinnamon
- 1 teaspoon maple flavoring
- 1/3 cup chopped nuts
- 6 tablespoons butter melted

GLAZE:

INGREDIENTS

- 1 1/2 cups powdered sugar
- 1/4 teaspoon maple flavoring
- 2–3 tablespoons milk

INSTRUCTIONS

1. Preheat oven to 370ºF.
2. Dissolve yeast in warm water from hot roll mix in large bowl.
3. Stir in egg, sugar, and maple flavoring.
4. Add hot roll flour mixture mixing well.
5. Knead on floured surface 2–3 minutes.
6. Place in greased bowl, cover, let rise until doubled in size (30–45 minutes).
7. Combine all filling ingredients except butter.
8. Grease 12-inch pizza pan. Divide dough into 3 equal balls. Roll one ball into 12-inch circle and fit into pizza pan.
9. Brush dough with 2 tablespoons melted butter and sprinkle with 1/3 cup filling.
10. Continue in same manner forming 2 more layers and ending with filling.
11. Use a glass to mark a 2-inch circle in center of dough; do not cut through.
12. Cut from outside edge just to circle forming 16 pie-shaped wedges.
13. Twist each of the 3 layered wedges 5 times.
14. Let rise in warm place until double in size 30–40 minutes.
15. Bake for 17 – 20 minutes or until golden brown.
16. Combine glaze ingredients until smooth and drizzle over coffee cake.

CPSIA information can be obtained
at www.ICGtesting.com
Printed in the USA
BVHW020252150922
647075BV00002BA/8